THE
WORSHIPPING CHURCH

Also available in the Pioneer *Perspectives* series:

Better Than or Equal To?	Linda Harding
Prophecy in the Church	Martin Scott
Radical Evangelism	Pete Gilbert
Relationships—Jesus Style	Stuart Lindsell
The Role and Ministry of Women	Martin Scott

For further information on the Pioneer *Perspectives* series and Pioneer, please write to:

P.O. Box 79c, Esher, Surrey, KT10 9LP

THE WORSHIPPING CHURCH

Noel Richards

WORD PUBLISHING

Word (UK) Ltd
Milton Keynes, England

WORD AUSTRALIA
Kilsyth, Victoria, Australia

WORD COMMUNICATIONS LTD
Vancouver, B.C., Canada

STRUIK CHRISTIAN BOOKS (PTY) LTD
Maitland, South Africa

CHRISTIAN MARKETING NEW ZEALAND LTD
Havelock North, New Zealand

JENSCO LTD
Hong Kong

JOINT DISTRIBUTORS SINGAPORE –
ALBY COMMERCIAL ENTERPRISES PTE LTD
and
CAMPUS CRUSADE

SALVATION BOOK CENTRE
Malaysia

THE WORSHIPPING CHURCH

© Pioneer 1993.

Published by Word (UK) Ltd. / Pioneer 1993.

ISBN 0-85009-730-4   (Australia ISBN 1-86258-249-1)

Printed in England by Clays Ltd, St Ives plc

93 94 95 96 / 10 9 8 7 6 5 4 3 2 1

FOREWORD

Pioneer *Perspectives* are perhaps more than their title suggests!

They are carefully researched presentations of material, on important issues, appealing to thinking churches, creative leaders and responsible Christians.

Each *Perspective* pioneers in as much as it is at the cutting edge of biblical and theological issues. Each will continue to pioneer with new ideas, concepts and data drawn from Scripture, history and a contemporary understanding of both.

They are perspectives in as much as they aim to be an important contribution to the ongoing debate on issues such as women in ministry and leadership; prophets and prophecy in the church; biblical models of evangelism; integrating and discipling new believers; growing and building local churches and further perspectives on Christ's second coming.

Importantly, these studies use a journal style of presentation, and are written by people who are currently working out the implications of the issues they are writing about, in local churches. This is vital if we are to escape the dangerous fantasy of abstract theology without practical experience. They are not written to contribute to the paralysis of analysis—rather to feed, strengthen, nurture and inform so that we can be equipped to get God's will done, by networking the nations with the gospel using all the resources that are available to us.

God's Word is always an event. How much we thank Him that He has left us an orderly account of what He wants us to believe, how He wants us to live, and what He wants us to do in order to bring heaven to the earth. As we embrace a better understanding of Scripture, rooted in local church, national and international mission, we shall become a part of the great eschatological purpose of bringing back the King—not for a church defeated, cowering and retiring but for one which, despite colossal odds, pressures and persecutions, is faithful to her Lord and His Word. To do that we must 'search the Scriptures' to see if many of these 'new things' are true. I commend these *Perspectives* to you as they are published on a regular basis throughout these coming years.

Gerald Coates
Director Pioneer Trust/Team Leader

Pioneer consists of a team and network of churches, committed to dynamic and effective biblical Christianity.

The national team act as advisers and consultants to churches, which in many cases develop into a partnership with the Pioneer team. These are the churches keen to identify with the theology, philosophy, ethos and purpose of Pioneer. The team have a vigorous youth ministry, church-planting strategy and evangelistic emphasis.

Training courses include Equipped to Lead, Emerging Leaders and the highly successful TIE teams (Training In Evangelism).

Pioneer have also been instrumental in initiating and funding March for Jesus (with Ichthus/YWAM); Jubilee Campaign (for the suffering church worldwide); and ACET (Aids Care Education Training).

ACKNOWLEDGEMENTS

I am grateful for all the people who have shaped my life over a period of many years. My parents and family provided an environment where I was able to discover God's love in a personal way.

Since then, friends too numerous to mention by name have invested good things into my life. This book would not be big enough to contain the list! I think about you often.

There are those to whom God has joined me in a specific way. I would not be what I am today without you all—my friends at Pioneer People, Cobham, those on the Pioneer Team and of course Gerald and Anona Coates. Gerald saw potential in me when my songs consisted mainly of clichéd lyrics such as 'died for me on Calvary to set me free'! He has shaped up my skills in writing, singing and leading in worship.

With regard to this book, special thanks go to Steve Clifford and Dave Roberts who took the time to read the manuscript and gave much advice on the content. Thanks also Steve for giving me much of the material for the 'developing team' section in Chapter 10.

Finally, special thanks go to my three best friends: my wife Tricia and children Sam and Amy.

Noel Richards
July 1992

CONTENTS

PREFACE

As a child, I found worship extremely tedious. I am grateful for the foundations that were put into my life by family and friends, but attending church three times every Sunday was hard work. My parents did allow me to take a book or drawing paper to meetings so that I would have something to occupy me. I am certain the thought passed through my mind that if Heaven is one long meeting, I was going to be bored for eternity. I contemplated the alternative but decided being bored was a more agreeable option!

My understanding of worship needed to change. As I grew out of childhood it did. It is so easy to regard worship as being what we do in the corporate setting of a church meeting. Worship though, is far greater than simply singing songs, praying and reading Scripture. Worship is about us offering our lives as a living sacrifice to our creator.

We are created to be worshippers. The Westminster Larger Catechism states that 'Man's chief end is to glorify God and fully to enjoy him forever.'

This book is a result of my own experiences as a worshipper and as one who has been privileged to lead others to a place of worship. It is a perspective based on what I have learned along the way. I have sought to make it as practical as possible and have tried to cover the subject in a broad way.

It is my sincere hope that as you read through these pages you will gain a fresh understanding of what it means to be a true worshipper, and of the role of worship in the life of the individual and the church.

I trust that it will also be a help to those who seek to lead others to a place of worship.

CHAPTER 1

THE OBJECT OF OUR WORSHIP

God, the creator of all things, is the object of our worship. He is the one who should be first in our affections. No one and nothing else is worthy to be worshipped. Jesus stated that the greatest commandment was to 'Love the Lord your God with all your heart and with all your soul and with all your mind' (Matt. 22:37). It was the first commandment given to the children of Israel.

We all have a capacity and a desire for worship. This desire is expressed in every human being. We worship what we love. Without God, we fill our lives with objects of affection that are substitutes for Him. Satan does not mind what we worship as long as it is not Jesus. Even as Christians we need to guard against God being someone who is tacked onto the end of our lives—someone who is regarded as an insurance policy against eternal judgement or who fits neatly into our schedule on Sundays only. Friends, children, career, hobbies, possessions can so easily replace God at the centre of our lives.

If our relationship with God is conducted on that basis, there is very little difference between us and someone who does not know Him.

Only one God

Every nation and people group expresses worship to some form of god. So many religions claim to offer a way to God, or true enlightenment. The uniqueness of Jesus Christ and the fact that He is the way, the truth and the life is continually challenged.

Christians believe there is only one God and that Jesus Christ is His only begotten Son—not merely a prophet ranking alongside those of other religions. He has, through His death and resurrection, provided the way to God. We must ensure that the God we worship is the God revealed to us through Scripture. He is not the product of a clever philosophy or the creation of someone who has suffered a grand delusion. He is 'the Lord God Almighty, who was, and is, and is to come (Rev. 4:8).

In spirit and in truth

Jesus made it clear that those who worship God do so in spirit and in truth (John 4:23,24). Under the old covenant, worship was performed in the tabernacle by a priesthood. Under the new covenant, we are the tabernacles or temples of the Holy Spirit. Where we worship is therefore irrelevant. Whether it be a cathedral or a mud hut is of no significance. The Lord does not live in houses made by men. When Heaven is your throne and earth your footstool, anything less is rather unimpressive! True worship must be in keeping with the nature of God, who is spirit. We therefore need to be filled with the Holy Spirit in order for this to happen.

In John's Gospel, truth is associated with Christ. We need to know Jesus who is the 'truth' in order to worship 'in truth'. This is important in our understanding of worship.

We also worship a God who can see through any pretence in our lives. He wants us to worship Him with honesty and reality.

God seeks worshippers

Also in John 4:23, we see that God the Father is seeking true worshippers. He looks for worshippers whose hearts are completely His. David was a man who failed God miserably at times. Yet he was a man of whom God could say: 'I have found David son of Jesse a man after my own heart' (Acts 13:22).

There is no deficiency in the Godhead. God is complete. What a privilege though, to be able to bring God pleasure and delight, when He has no need of anything that we could give.

Falling in love again

Jesus is passionately in love with His bride the church. He longs for the day when He will present us before His Father. For the joy of this, He went to the cross, in order to save us and draw us to Himself (Heb. 12:2,3).

Jesus has done more for us than anyone else ever could. In His death, He took upon Himself all the consequences of our sin. When the realisation of that fact hits us, our only response is to fall in love with Him.

Every relationship goes through the 'honeymoon' phase. Everything is wonderful. Before very long however, disillusionment creeps in. This is a critical stage because we are then faced with two options. One is to end the relationship, the other is to choose to hold on to the relationship and work through the disillusionment.

Jesus never gets disillusioned with us because He had no illusions in the first place. However, through the ups and downs of life we may find that we have lost that sparkle in our friendship with the Lord. We may feel that we are not doing enough for Him, that we have let Him down in some way. If sin has found its way into our lives, that will be a continual barrier unless we confess it and receive forgiveness. Sometimes we can be so busy serving Jesus that we lose sight of why we are doing it in the first place.

At times like this we need to rediscover the love that we have for the Lord. If we are so busy doing things for God that we have no time for Him, we must re-examine our priorities. Jesus wants our lives, not our usefulness. He loves us, not our achievements.

Let's get back to first base—to the place of intimacy with the One who loves us, where we enjoy Him and He enjoys us.

CHAPTER 2

WORSHIP IS A LIFESTYLE

Therefore, I urge you, brothers, in view of God's mercy, to offer your bodies as living sacrifices, holy and pleasing to God—this is your spiritual act of worship.

Romans 12:1

It would be impossible to write a book on worship without this fundamental chapter. What happens in our meetings is pointless if we do not understand what worship is. If we think that worship is what happens on a Sunday morning or evening, we have not even started!

We should not be switching into worship mode when we go to a church meeting. Worship is for life, not just for meetings. Everything we do needs to be seen as an act of worship. Worship should encompass the whole of our lives. We were created with a capacity for worship. It is a basic part of our nature.

Jesus spoke of the need for reality in our worship (John 4:24). He was not concerned with the externals. Rather, he was concerned with what was going on in the heart of the worshipper. He is not merely interested in the songs we sing, but the lives we lead.

The quality of the worship we experience in our church is related to the quality of the worshippers. Corporate worship is a reflection of individual worship. Worship leaders cannot motivate nonworshippers to worship.

God wants us to develop a lifestyle of worship. Let

us consider some of the areas of our lives that affect the credibility of our worship.

Relationships

It is vital that we have a right relationship with our brothers and sisters. Relationship and community is at the heart of the Godhead. God the Father, God the Son and God the Holy Spirit dwell in harmony together. At the beginning of time, God stated that it is not good for man to be alone. He has given us each other and we belong to His family. It is difficult to bless God when we are in conflict with a member of this family. Our offering of worship is soured by disunity (Matt. 5:23, 24).

1 John 4:20 tells us we are liars if we claim to love God yet hate a brother or sister. The Bible does not pull its punches.

God commands blessing on those who dwell in unity (Ps. 133:1–3).

Speech

Words are powerful. They can be creative or destructive, a blessing or a curse. We can never take them back once they have been spoken. I guess we all wish we could at one time or another. Scripture tells us that it is absurd to be slandering someone one moment and then be trying to bless God the next (James 3:9–12).

Actions

Sin is no longer an inevitability because we have been regenerated and empowered by the Holy Spirit (1 John 2:1). There may be times, however, when we find sin has crept in through the 'back door', for whatever reason. It is then that we either choose to confess or cover up. If we confess to God and to one another, light comes into our lives. We do not fear being found out and the issue is dealt with. Our relationship with God is restored and worship can flow.

Obedience

In 1 Samuel 15, Saul was instructed to destroy the Amalekites and all they had. Saul disobeyed the Lord: he spared their king and kept the best sheep and cattle. When confronted by Samuel, Saul lied, saying that God's command had been obeyed. 'What then is this bleating of sheep in my ears?' asks Samuel. Saul's excuse was that he intended to sacrifice the animals to the Lord. 'To obey is better than sacrifice,' declared Samuel.

The sound of the 'bleating sheep' of disobedience will drown out the sound of our worship.

Heart attitude

I grew up in the Pentecostal tradition. Our leaders did not dress up in robes but there was an acceptable way to dress if you were coming to worship. We would frown at anyone who came to a meeting dressed in a biker's jacket and jeans. We were certainly concerned with externals. As if God was interested in how much our suits cost!

We can be so judgemental of people when it comes to worship. Do they wear the right clothes, do they dance, do they raise their hands, do they 'speak in tongues'? We judge whether or not a person is a worshipper by whether or not they perform in a way that conforms to our expectations.

God however, looks into our hearts and not the external appearance we present. Are they filled with gratitude towards Him? Are we generous towards Him and others? Do we give Him the best, or does He take second place in our affections? Is there any cynicism that robs God, others and ourselves of blessing? Are we proud or walking in humility? Do we desire to serve or seek leadership for our own gain? This is what God looks at when we worship Him.

Praising God continually

Religion tells us that we must have 'quiet times' with God. Religion tells us that God only accepts us on the basis of what we do for Him.

God is not interested in 'quiet times' based on a legalistic duty. He wants a relationship based on our response to His love for us. If we have a daily 'check-in' with the Almighty, motivated by a fear that we are in trouble if we don't, nothing will be achieved.

If I was God, I would be less than satisfied with a relationship where someone gave me fifteen minutes in the morning, out of a sense of duty. Indeed, I could not envisage relating to my wife or children in that way.

The good news is that we can enjoy God continually. The communication channels are always open. We can experience His presence in every circumstance of life (Heb. 13:15).

Wherever we are and whatever we are doing, we can offer up praise and thanksgiving to the Lord. We can give to Him and hear from Him twenty-four hours a day.

Each of us is different though. To some, a special time to meet with God is important. For others, that approach would be less than helpful.

Carrying the presence of God

I believe you can tell, within a very short time of meeting someone, whether or not they are a worshipper. We all give off the atmosphere in which we live. In my work I travel quite extensively and have stayed in many homes. In some homes I have sensed I am with a family who love the Lord. In others, I cannot wait to get away!

I remember staying in the home of Arthur and Eileen Wallis several years ago. Arthur was one of the key figures in the 'house church' movement. Of all the hundreds of homes I have stayed in during the last twenty years, theirs made a lasting impression on me. I was aware of the presence of God both in their lives and in their home.

I sang in a number of wine bars back in early 1982. One owner eventually offered me the prime evening slot because, as he put it, 'There is a different atmosphere in the place when you are around.' I was not singing about Jesus. I was singing classic pop songs. However, we can take the presence of God with us into every situation.

Let us endeavour to involve God in every area of our lives and allow Him to make His presence felt in everything we do. We want our worship to have the integrity of being rooted in a lifestyle that is consistent with the values of the Kingdom.

CHAPTER 3

THE POWER OF PRAISE

Praise marches

In May 1987, 15,000 Christians from all denominations gathered in the pouring rain at London's Smithfield Meat Market.

They were participating in an event called 'The City March'. The organisers of the event were Roger Forster(Ichthus), Lynn Green (YWAM), Gerald Coates (Pioneer) and Graham Kendrick.

They marched from the market into the City of London, the heart of finance. They asked God to show people the foolishness of trusting in riches, rather than Himself. Within months, scandal rocked the financial institutions and in October 1987 came the stock exchange crash. This heralded the end of the affluent (for some) eighties. A coincidence or an answer to prayer?

Prayer and praise is powerful. I am sure we have experienced the truth of this in our own lives. When God's people take prayer and praise onto the streets, spiritual strangleholds are broken. Satan is the prince of the power of the air but God inhabits the praises of His people (Psalm 22:3 AV). As we march and praise, God is with us, just as He was when the Israelites carried the ark in Old Testament days. Therefore as we praise march through our towns and cities, we bring God's presence to the streets, changing the atmosphere and driving back the powers of darkness.

In the mid 1980s, Roger Forster led several praise marches into Soho, London's red-light area. They prayed that Soho would become a clean place and that the Holy Spirit would drive out unclean spirits. A short time later, the whole area was raided by the police and every illegal sex show was shut down. To Roger's knowledge, this had never happened before or since.

There are examples of praise linked with warfare in Scripture. In 2 Chronicles 20:21–23 we see the results of this. As Jehosophat sent a group of people into the enemy territory, praising God, that enemy became confused and destroyed itself.

Satan seeks to destroy the lives of people who are loved by their Creator. Praise is one of the weapons the church has at its disposal, to defeat him. The final victory has been decided through Jesus, but there are still battles to be fought and won.

Psalm 149 speaks of having praise in the mouth and a sword in the hand. Words have much power. The words of truth that we sing and speak in faith become powerful weapons. They will overcome Satan's lies.

Praise changes our situations

It is easy to praise God when everything is going well. When we go through the difficult periods, questions often replace worship. I am not one who believes in praising God *for* my circumstances. Especially if I do not feel thankful for them.

That to me is unreality. My attitude is that I will praise God *in* my circumstances. 1 Thessalonians 5:18 encourages us to do this. Our joy is not dependent on circumstances but comes from the Lord. Though our situations change, He does not. He is always worthy of our worship.

Praise is powerful! Look at the results of praise in Acts 16. Paul and Silas chose to praise God in hopeless circumstances and some dramatic changes took place.

Firstly, they began to see the prison from God's perspective. As they worshipped the Lord, they began to realise how big and powerful He is. Mere walls are no problem to a God who can conquer death.

Secondly, their faith began to rise. This will always happen when we choose to praise God. Praise is like switching a light on in a darkened room. We can then see our problems for what they are. Fear of the unknown is replaced by faith.

Thirdly, the circumstances changed. An earthquake destroyed the prison. A coincidence—or was this God intervening in the situation? I believe it was the latter. I have met with people who received physical healing while praising God. When faith is released in worship, anything is possible!

I am sure Paul and Silas encouraged each other to worship. We need to encourage one another to worship. Look out for those who are struggling in circumstances and use the words of Psalm 34:3: 'Glorify the Lord with me: let us exalt his name together.'

You may have come across groups of Christians who refuse to participate in 'praise/prayer marches'. They claim that praying on the streets is unscriptural. I do not know what kind of Bible they read! Anyone with a basic understanding of the New Testament will know that the early church was far more visible than it is today. There was a lot of 'on the street' activity.

CHAPTER 4

WORSHIP AND MUSIC

Worship is musical

God loves music and there are countless musical references throughout Scripture. We have the Book of Psalms, the Song of Solomon and whole passages of Scripture that would have been sung. From reading Revelation we see that music plays an important role in the age to come.

The Old Testament prophets worked with musicians who stirred up their prophetic gifts: 1 Samuel 10:5, 2 Kings 3:14–15, 1 Chronicles 25:1–3. In Numbers 10:9, we see music as a prayer to God. Zephaniah 3:17 speaks of the Lord rejoicing over us with singing. Habakkuk chapter 3 is a prayer that appears to have been used as a Psalm.

Music has always played a significant role in worship and will continue to do so. Psalm 47:6 exhorts us to sing praises to God. Psalms 81, 98 and 150 detail the immense range of musical instruments that can be used in worship.

Stringed, wind and percussive instruments give us a lot of scope. Unlike some Christians I occasionally encounter, God does not have a problem with drums and different rhythms. I heard of one church where the leaders were against drums in worship because they were not mentioned in the Bible. On that absurd basis, we should never use the lavatory, since it is not mentioned in Scripture that Jesus ever did! I have even heard of some Christians having problems with clapping or playing drums on the off-beat. Tell that to your average black gospel choir member!

What style of music?

God enjoys all styles of music!

Most Christians' problems with the style of music and instruments used in worship are cultural ones. They try to 'spiritualise' their own cultural preference rather than honestly admit their dislike of a certain style. Some styles of music leave me absolutely cold. They do nothing for me. However, other people would enjoy those styles and feel able to worship while using them.

God created music and it is a neutral medium. It is neither good nor bad. While some use music as a vehicle for worship, others use it for idolatrous purposes. This is true of every style of music, from classical to heavy metal. Let's not forget that many of the classical composers were as debauched as the pop musicians of today. It is the motivation behind music that is important, not the style. I long to see Christian musicians and artistes emerging who will bring a new content and 'spirit' to the music industry.

Let's explore different styles of music in our worship. In our own church on one particular Sunday we had everything from the contemporary 'house' style music to a traditional hymn. Some churches use chants and unaccompanied singing. God is a God of variety and there is room for musical variety in our worship.

Old songs or new songs?

Scripture encourages us to 'sing a new song' to the Lord. I can see two main reasons for doing so.

Firstly, our worship reflects our attitude to what God is currently saying to us, both individually and corporately. It is also a means of communicating the current emphasis to the church. A decade ago, God was challenging the church on unity. We sang songs such as 'Bind us together'. In the '90s, the emphasis seems to be on the church's great commission. What we are singing now should reflect this. A church that is responding to the current prophetic emphasis will be introducing new songs. Those that are not, only sing the 'good old hymns'.

Secondly, the reason why we sing new songs is that we get tired of singing the same ones over and over again. Unless they are timeless 'classics' many of the songs we are currently singing will have a very short 'shelf-life'. I am sure we all know songs that when introduced, were being sung almost every week, but now are only sung occasionally.

The 'traditional' hymns we have today were the 'popular' songs of yesterday. Many of them were radical and prophetic in their own time and some outstanding ones still are. Some of these songs were frowned upon and seen as unacceptable for worship. An example of this is 'Onward Christian Soldiers' which was considered as militant and not solemn enough when first written. In fact a lot of the early Salvation Army songs were based on tunes which were used in the drinking dens of the day.

Eventually, the 'popular' songs became acceptable and then over a longer period became 'traditional'. The same will happen to many of the new songs we are singing in our churches today.

Singing reality

I love singing songs of exuberant praise and being in events where we celebrate God's goodness together.

It is easy though to come into a worship meeting or celebration event and escape from the real world and all its pressures. I have at times been disturbed by the fact that we can watch world events unfolding on our TV screens and not make any reference to them during our meetings. Thousands may have perished in a natural disaster, yet we still sing 'Jesus we celebrate your victory' (one of my all-time favourite songs).

God is always deserving of the highest praise, no matter what is happening in the world. Yet we need to earth that praise in an acknowledgement of reality. The most casual glance at the Book of Psalms will give us another perspective on what we can express in song to our Lord. The following are some examples:

Sorrow: Psalm 6.
Cry for help: Psalm 12, 69.
Cry for vengeance: Psalm 109.
Repentance: Psalm 51.
Security: Psalm 62.
Complaint: Psalm 22.
Petition: Psalm 17.

The Psalms cater for every experience of life and express the reality of how it is for many of us as we gather to worship.

Contrast Psalm 22 with Psalm 136 as one example of the diversity expressed. Where Psalm 22 complains about being forsaken by God, Psalm 136 speaks of God's love enduring for ever.

Looking through any traditional hymn book we will find songs for every occasion. The challenge for those of us who are writing today's hymns and songs is that we should cover the range of human emotions. We should write songs that deal with despair, bereavement and anxiety, to name but a few, yet point the singer to the God who is changeless and worthy of worship.

While the Gulf War was in progress, my home church decided it would be inappropriate to sing songs of warfare in our public meetings. We did not want to be seen as a people who glory in warfare—albeit spiritual—by those unchurched who may have been visiting us. Likewise when Graham Kendrick and I led worship at a prayer meeting for the Gulf crisis, in February 1991 at London's Royal Albert Hall, we chose our songs carefully. So many of the praise songs we sing could be interpreted as being pro-Jewish—and therefore anti-Arab—by the media.

Singing in the Spirit

This is when our singing is motivated by and in co-operation with the Holy Spirit. In 1 Corinthians 14:15, Paul speaks of two distinct areas of singing in the Spirit:

1. Singing with the Spirit

This is when we bypass our understanding and sing in our 'tongues' language. It may be a song of praise, a prayer or something prophetic which will be interpreted.

Sometimes our attitude to worship can be that we have reached the 'climax' when people are 'singing in tongues'. This burst of tongues lasts for a short while and then it is over. Why do we not sing in tongues for a longer period than that? Why not start off a period of worship by singing for several minutes in tongues instead of our native language? How about singing in the major and the minor keys and being a lot more creative with the music?

2. Singing with the mind

This is when we sing creatively in our native tongue using our understanding. We do not see enough of this. We can become comfortable singing from our song-books and then singing in tongues. However, in making that leap, we miss out on a wonderful area of creative worship.

When I lead worship, I often encourage people to sing in their native language what they are feeling towards the Lord. With my musicians I provide a simple melody on which people can sing out phrases of love and adoration. Songs that express praise, worship, feelings and responses to God.

Singing with the mind involves us in creative thought. When singing with the Spirit it is easier to slip into an automatic response. It might be a useful exercise to see how long we can sing with our minds before we exhaust our vocabulary and need to resort to 'singing in tongues'.

Singing with understanding

Do we really understand all the lyrics of the hymns and songs that we use? Years ago, I remember singing the song 'Let's go up to Zion'. I do not recall ever stopping to think what that meant. Where is Zion? What does it mean to 'go up to Zion'? The lyrics were in one sense immaterial. It had a strong melody line and we enjoyed singing it. It always went down well with the congregation.

We need to pay attention to the lyrics we sing. Are they written in language and terminology we can relate to? Or do we need a concordance to understand them? Do the singers know what they are singing?

Are the songs theologically correct? Many Christians get their theology from songs rather than Scripture. Do the words fall glibly from our lips? It happens so easily, particularly with well-known songs. We can sing them without putting the brain into gear. Sometimes it is good to pause in the middle of a time of worship and, before singing a familiar song, take a fresh look at the words.

CHAPTER 5

WORSHIP AND PHYSICAL EXPRESSION

A friend of mine was once criticised regarding the worship at his church meetings. He was told the worship was 'fleshly'. 'Absolutely right,' was his reply. 'I do not have an out-of-the-body experience when I worship God!' We cannot divorce worship from physical expression. Worship was never meant to be 'cerebral', something that merely touches our intellect. Our worship of God involves our whole being (Deut. 6: 5).

Cerebral worship produces nothing but passivity. God is bored with that, in the same way that our wives/husbands would be bored if we only loved each other with our minds.

Whenever we see someone dancing in worship, we label that person 'extrovert'. I would see that person as normal. In Britain, we are afraid of our bodies and of using them for physical expression. We refrain from embracing someone of the same sex for fear of being regarded as homosexual. Men who cry are considered weak. We still suffer from the Victorian legacy of the 'stiff upper lip'. We are afraid to show our true feelings and that affects our worship.

True worship involves abandoning our whole being to God—our hearts, minds and bodies. Anything less is sterile and religious.

God is a passionate lover and we can reciprocate that love with an equal amount of passion.

Let us examine what the Bible says about various forms of 'physical' worship.

Dance

The story of the Ark being brought to Jerusalem in 2 Samuel 6:12–23 is a wonderful picture of worship. David, full of joy that God's anger had been appeased, 'danced before the Lord with all his might' (v. 14). That phrase speaks to me of dancing that was powerful, masculine and sensual. This was no 'Charismatic Hop'. Indeed it was offensive to his wife, who seemed to have little spiritual understanding. Michal called his dancing 'vulgar'. How often I have heard that response from nonworshippers who criticise dancing in worship.

Ecclesiastes 3:4 says there is a time to mourn and a time to dance. There are times when our worship will be full of weeping and not celebration. We will not feel like dancing all the time. However, the Lord can turn our mourning into dancing (Psalm 30:11).

The children of Israel danced and praised God when they had been delivered from the oppression of Egypt (Exodus 15:21). Sometimes we will be so happy that the only thing we can do is jump for joy. Psalm 149:3 says: 'Let them praise his name with dancing.'

Dancing, like every other expression of worship, has been hijacked by Satan. He causes dancing to be something that brings glory to self and not the Creator or, by being erotic, attracts a sexual encounter.

For that reason, people feel safer with so-called 'sacred dancing' that is mainly ballet style. However, there are people who get sexually stimulated by ballet. The problem is often the watcher's, not the dancer's.

The dancing we have in our meetings will range from fun and enjoyment, through praise, to intensely powerful expressions of intimacy with our Father. It is easy for these expressions to be misread or misunderstood by an onlooker. But that is not a sufficient reason to stop people from dancing in our meetings.

Don't limit dancing in praise and worship to a particular style. Everyone dances differently. I have seen people throwing cart-wheels during praise and worship.

At other times I have seen people dance with partners. In a celebration-style event, it has not seemed inappropriate.

On a final point, some people say that dancing is not for the New Testament Christian, because we only read of dancing in the Old Testament. If people danced in Old Testament times before Christ had come, how much more should we be dancing, now that there is forgiveness of sins, peace with God and a hope of eternal life! We do not need to be told to dance, we cannot help but dance! Let us also remember that dancing is a part of real life. Everyone dances. People with miserable, Godless lives dance. Christians have this idea that if we dance we are 'free'. If we are dancing in our meetings, it does not mean we are free, we are normal! Colossians 3:16 encourages us to sing the Psalms, bringing Old Testament worship into our New Testament experience. Psalm 149 encourages us to 'praise his name with dancing'.

Bowing down and kneeling

A common expression in the Scriptures is 'bowed' or 'fell down and worshipped' (Gen. 24:48; Exod. 4:31; Job 1:20; Matt. 2:11, 28:9; Rev. 11:16, 19:4). The Greek and Hebrew words that are used for praise and worship speak of physical expression. They often paint the picture of falling down before the Lord and kissing His feet in intimate adoration, such as in Luke 7:36–50.

Psalm 5:7 speaks of bowing down in reverence and Psalm 95:6 encourages us to bow down in worship and kneel before the Lord our maker. Bowing is an expression of honour, submission and repentance.

In Ezra 9:5 the writer falls on his knees as he is aware that guilty people cannot stand in the presence of the Lord (v. 15).

I have been in worship meetings where the presence of God is so powerful that men and women have fallen flat on their faces before Him.

Clapping

We are used to applauding a good concert or the skill of a sportsman. People receive 'standing ovations' for giving an excellent performance.

We need to make room in our meetings for applauding the Lord. I recall being at a large celebration attended by around 2,000 people. There was a 50-piece orchestra leading the worship. At the end of one song the congregation burst into applause, which petered out after around 30 seconds.

The leader of the event informed everyone that he reckoned God was worth more applause than that. We then gave the Lord around five minutes of applause accompanied by the orchestra—particularly the percussionists. It was powerful!

Psalm 47:1 says, 'Clap your hands . . . shout to God with cries of joy.' Let's have a lot more clapping and shouts of joy in our worship times.

As well as applause, we can clap as we sing, using our hands as percussion instruments.

Raising hands

Psalm 134:2 says, 'Lift up your hands . . . and praise the Lord.' Hands are so expressive when it comes to worship. As we raise our hands we can be saying: I surrender, I receive, I worship, I give. Go to any football match or pop concert and you will see the use of raised hands in praise, adoration and worship.

I find it sad that Christians can go to these sorts of events and have no problem raising their hands to 'human gods', yet criticise a worship leader who encourages the raising of hands in a meeting.

Paul in his letter to Timothy encouraged the lifting up of hands in prayer (1 Tim. 2:8).

Shouting

Psalm 98:4 says, 'Shout for joy to the Lord, all the earth.' We are going to see a lot more shouting in our meetings. Shouts of joy, praise and warfare. Noise is a sign of life. A quiet church is a dead church!

The Lord loves shouting; He does it. In Isaiah 42:13 it says 'with a shout he will raise the battle cry'. No army goes into battle quietly. They make as much noise as they can in order to intimidate the enemy. The Lord is a warrior and His church is a warrior church. We are made for battle. In our meetings, particularly our prayer meetings, let's raise a loud battle cry with our high praises. Maybe we should rename our prayer meetings and call them 'war meetings'.

CHAPTER 6

WORSHIP AND PROPHECY

Worship is two-way communication, not one-way. As we bring our offering of praise and worship to the Lord, I am sure He wants to be given room to respond. God loves to share His heart with us, if only we will take the time to listen. Zephaniah 3:17 states that God will rejoice over us with singing. I have often asked people to listen to the song God wants to sing to them as individuals, while the musicians continue to play.

It seems to me that some Christians are afraid of silence. They fill every space in a meeting with another song. It is good for a worship leader to leave space for silent worship. However, there is a risk that someone, somewhere in the congregation will jump in and insensitively rattle off an inappropriate prophetic word.

An example of this was a conference I once attended. There were several hundred church leaders present. I had given careful and prayerful thought to the event and how I should lead the worship. We reached a point in the evening where people were on their knees, some weeping. It was evident God was moving among us. I have learnt that at these times it is best to do nothing and let the Holy Spirit do what He wants. There was a holy silence on the gathering. Suddenly, someone began to sing, 'Be still for the presence of the Lord, the holy one is here.' We did not need someone to sing at that point. We were aware of the presence of the Lord and we were being still! It was totally inappropriate. I literally felt the Holy Spirit evaporating from the meeting. He is easily grieved. I spoke with some of the leaders of that event later. I discovered they had been inundated with people queueing up to give 'prophetic' words during that time. None had been allowed to get near a microphone because the so-called prophecies were little more than 'blessed thoughts'. Correct, but hardly prophetic.

This may sound a little judgemental but we are told to weigh prophecy carefully (1 Cor. 14:29). I believe we need to do this both before and after a word is given. Prophecy is not something to be taken lightly. A prophetic word is not there in our worship meetings as another ingredient to make a 'good time of worship'. If it is a truly prophetic word, it is God, speaking personally to us. We need to discern the difference between God speaking and an emotional outburst.

When the Holy Spirit moves in a time of corporate worship, there is an unlocking of the prophetic gift. Leadership needs to handle this carefully. Paul, speaking in 1 Corinthians 14:29, stated that at the most, only three prophets should speak. This does not mean that if we have four words next Sunday we are in error. Paul was being practical. There is only so much the mind can take in. If we have fourteen prophetic words in a meeting, how many will we remember and give attention too? Prophetic words must be taken seriously. They are not 'charismatic' entertainment.

The role of musicians and singers

Since Old Testament times it has been recognised that musicians have a role in unlocking the prophetic.

In 1 Samuel 10:5 we read: 'As you approach the town, you will meet a procession of prophets coming down from the high place with lyres, tambourines, flutes and harps being played before them, and they will be prophesying.'

Elisha the prophet knew the power of music in stirring the prophetic gift. We read in 2 Kings 3:14–15 that he called for a harpist. As the musician played, the hand of the Lord came upon Elisha and he prophesied.

King David called together a large group of people for the ministry of prophesying, accompanied by harps, lyres and cymbals (1 Chron. 25:1–7). He himself was a prophetic psalmist, Psalm 22 being an example of him moving in this gift.

In my worship team, I include those who have a gift in the area of prophetic singing. These are people who feel more comfortable singing a prophetic message rather than speaking it. A song can sometimes be more powerful than a sermon. People often forget much of what the preacher said in a 35-minute talk, but they remember the song that crystallised that message.

My prophetic singers practise constantly. They develop vocal skills and the ability to form phrases quickly from a basic idea. Sometimes, all they will get from the Holy Spirit is one simple thought. As they come to the microphone, they may only have one line of the prophetic song. It is a real step of faith. Usually, as they begin to sing, the rest of the song follows.

Writing prophetic songs

Tricia, my wife, who writes worship songs with me, goes a little further. She keeps a notebook of songs that God gives her. Some are no more than a few lines. On paper they do not look that special. However, when the Holy Spirit prompts her to share one of these songs, a new dynamic is at work and the words carry power. She also comes to public meetings with blank overhead projector slides. As a prophetic song comes to her during the course of the meeting, she writes the lyrics on the slide. When she sings the song, the lyrics can then be projected for all the congregation to see. This enables them to join in with the singing of the song.

In order for this to work effectively, the singers and musicians need to have a close rapport. In our worship team practices, we make room for singing spontaneous songs. In that way, all my musicians learn how to flow with prophetic singing.

Finally, I want to encourage songwriters to 'sit at the feet' of those with prophetic ministries. They have a role to play in taking the words of the prophets and condensing them into easily remembered songs. These prophetic songs will be sung, even where the prophet is not accepted.

I have been privileged to work with Gerald Coates during the last ten years. His preaching is prophetic and has inspired much of my songwriting. I have endeavoured to capture what God is saying and put it into worship/praise songs. As the church worships with these songs, they are declaring the current prophetic emphasis. Having this prophetic element in our worship is vital. Songs are one of the simplest ways of teaching people. These prophetic songs therefore enable the whole church to grasp what is in God's heart for His people.

CHAPTER 7

WORSHIP AND LITURGY

What is liturgy?

Quite simply, liturgy is a fixed form of public worship used in church.

Every denominational grouping has a liturgy in their worship. The charismatic 'house churches' or 'newer churches', which is a more appropriate description, have always prided themselves on their lack of liturgy and free worship. Yet they do have a liturgy, which in its simplest form is usually an hour of worship followed by an hour of teaching. There is plenty of *life* in their liturgy but very little *content*. For instance, there has been a real lack of hymnology that draws attention to the needs of the world.

The reason for the life is that these churches make room for the Holy Spirit. They do not want to recite liturgical phrases week in, week out. They have a dynamic approach to worship that involves the gifts of the Holy Spirit. There is prophetic singing, singing in tongues and room for the spontaneous. The songs are from the pen of modern writers and emphasise what God is currently saying to the church. Worship is not sacramental and is very informal.

All this is good but there is very little creativity involved. The meetings can become boring because the same thing happens each week. Being spontaneous in worship can lead to spontaneous nothing. There is a fear of symbolism and a lack of credal statements.

However, I far prefer the much freer liturgy that we

now have in these churches to the liturgy that exists in, say, the Church of England. Although powerful and full of wonderful truths, I could not sit through that every week! There is plenty of *content* in the liturgy but very little *life*.

The basic reason for the absence of life is not the liturgy. It is the absence of leadership that creates room for the Holy Spirit to move. The third person of the Trinity is stifled. Little emotion is aroused, and it is even frowned upon. It is worship that touches the head but not the heart.

Another reason for its lack of life is that the liturgy is couched in classical English language. It is a quaint museum piece. It is totally meaningless to your average person on the street. The worship is alienated from culture. Even the hymns require a dictionary to be understood. They are musically and lyrically out of date. For example:

> *Crown him the Lord of life*
> *The potentate of time*
> *Creator of the rolling spheres*
> *Ineffably sublime.*

A wonderful classic hymn in its day and I do enjoy singing it. Yet it uses language that is not in everyday use. What do lines two, three and four mean, without resorting to a dictionary?

There was a time when the culture of a nation changed slowly. It was therefore unnecessary for constant change in the style and format of church meetings. However, we are seeing changes in our culture at an accelerating rate. A style of music that is 'in' today is irrelevant tomorrow.

The church cannot ignore cultural change, unless it wants to become irrelevant.

It is tragic that as society approaches the twenty-first century, most churches' public meetings are at best locked into an early twentieth-century culture.

We cannot afford the luxury of maintaining a style

of liturgy that we find therapeutic and culturally preferable. There is a world to evangelise that does not relate to eighteenth-century language, traditional hymns and all the religious paraphernalia that goes into church services. If you like all of that, enjoy it in private but the public face of the church must change.

Most of the large celebration-style events that I participate in are no longer modelled on the traditional approach. Most people seem to prefer the latest worship songs, a non-religious approach and an informal liturgy. It is a tragedy that some of these people have to go home to 'museum-style' worship after events of this nature.

We must take the wonderful expressions of truth in our liturgies and up-date them. There must be a way to re-work liturgy so that its content can be appreciated by a new generation. Make it relevant once again.

Our music must change and incorporate the new, no matter how sentimental we feel about a certain style. There are some within the established churches who look down on the 'charismatic ditties' being sung in the newer churches. Yet that is where the life is and growth is happening. The traditional churches, apart from some notable exceptions, are losing members at an alarming rate.

I have visited a church in Switzerland that has three services on a Sunday. The first morning service is the more traditional type of gathering. Its liturgy reflects the needs of the older members of the church, who turn out in force. The remaining two services have a modern liturgy and appeal to the younger members, who are in the majority. In taking this approach, they are relevant to this generation while providing something for those who prefer tradition.

Holy Trinity Brompton in London is a major Anglican church that is combining the new with the old. Their worship is fresh and they have caught a vision of what God is doing now.

At St Peter's and St Paul's Anglican church in Swanley, Kent, they have a non-religious building, a contemporary approach to worship and a growing congregation.

I hope these comments will encourage us all to look at the way we worship in the light of our great commission—to evangelise the world. The church that I am part of has had to do a radical re-think of what our public meetings should be like. We have made changes because we want our worship times to be sensitive to those whom we are trying to reach with the gospel.

Is our liturgy flexible?

The above observations are for every church. We all need to look at the way our church worships. We are creatures of habit and we dislike change. Yet a church that does not constantly re-evaluate its liturgy is likely to become more and more irrelevant.

Our liturgy of songs, prayers, Scripture readings, and so on is simply scaffolding on which our worship is built. Scaffolding is known as 'temporary works'. It is there to facilitate the building programme, not hinder it. Unfortunately, the 'scaffolding' of our Sunday morning/ evening liturgy can remain the same, for years on end. It becomes cherished and to suggest changing it is tantamount to heresy. I often ask people why they have two church meetings on a Sunday. Is it because of tradition or because it is a 'model' that is working for them?

Our liturgy must be the kind that is subject to the Holy Spirit so that we can give God what He desires and deserves.

Anything less is just a lot of activity. We cannot ask the Holy Spirit to honour our meetings with His presence and then dictate to Him how we want Him to behave.

Charismatic v. non-charismatic worship

We must get out of the mind-set that causes us to think that worship is for our benefit and blessing.

What God is receiving is the issue. Anything we receive is a bonus. If God is not enjoying our offering of worship, we need to ask why. The difficulty is that my opinion of what God likes will be different to another person's opinion.

That is why we must allow the Holy Spirit to have freedom in our meetings. He is the one who enables us to worship our Creator. He will not lead us into unbiblical confusion and error. Anything that does, is not the Holy Spirit. To give the Holy Spirit freedom in our meetings does not mean that every Sunday we will be singing wild songs and 'swinging from the chandeliers'! There will be times of repentance, weeping, silence, celebration and adoration.

Whenever I lead worship at events there are those who feel threatened by 'charismatic worship'. Because I use the newer songs as opposed to the traditional hymns they claim the worship is too 'charismatic'. There is a basic misunderstanding. They think that if I sing traditional hymns the worship will not be 'charismatic'.

Charismatic worship occurs not because of modern songs but when the Holy Spirit moves upon us and energises our offering to God.

That can just as easily occur while we are singing traditional hymns.

Every church needs to be 'charismatic' in its approach to meetings. There is not another option. We either welcome the Holy Spirit and give Him permission to do what He wants, or we have a church that pleases people, not God.

As a worship leader, my priority is to honour the

Holy Spirit and lead the congregation where I feel He wants me to. I am aware that in doing so, a lot of people (particularly in a traditional church) could be offended, or filled with fear. I therefore believe that God asks me to take people forward in ways they can cope with. To treat them with sensitivity and love is an expression of my love for God. It may take a little time to move people forward but God is patient. He seeks to win people. The Holy Spirit is a gentleman, not a bully, and I must remember that.

CHAPTER 8

PREPARING FOR WORSHIP MEETINGS

We are creative

God is creative and we have been given the ability to express creativity in all aspects of our lives.

God's creativity is:

1. **Excellent**: Gen. 1:4, 10, 12, 18, 21, 25, 31; 1 Tim. 4:4. What God made was good.
2. **Extravagant**: Gen. 1:11, 12, 14–16, 20, 21, 24, 25; Psalm 104. God created an abundance of everything. He is not mean.
3. **Ordered**: Gen. 1:1; Job 38:4–14. When God created the world, He produced order out of chaos.
4. **Colourful**: Look at all the wonderful colours, shapes, textures and fragrances that God has created.
5. **Beautiful**: Matt. 6:28, 29.
6. **Dramatic**: Thunderstorms, earthquakes, fire, wind, water.

Creativity will lead us to the Creator. It communicates something of His nature to us. A flower has no need of a Scripture verse on it in order for it to reflect something of God. Likewise, our acts of creativity can point people towards the Lord. Learning to be creative in everyday life will enable us to be more creative in our times of corporate worship.

However, creativity should not become a substitute

for the Holy Spirit in our meetings. Let's use our creative abilities in partnership with the Holy Spirit's inspiration. Let's not pursue creativity as the means of making our worship meetings better. People giving themselves in worship will do that.

What are we meeting for?

This question must be asked each time we get together as a church—from a small home group to a large celebration event, and everything in between.

We need to view the whole of the meeting as an act of worship. Preaching, praying, Bible reading, singing, are all expressions of worship. Even the 'notices'! Let us not view the singing as worship and the remainder as non-worship activity. People who contribute to the meeting with drama, dance, poetry and other creative activities are also expressing worship. However, we recognise that within this act of worship there is what has become known as a 'time of worship'. I do not know of anything else that it could be called. This is when we sing together and express the praise and adoration that are on our hearts.

The purpose of the meeting will determine the length of time that we give to this activity. It will also help us decide the level of response we are expecting in that time. What is appropriate in a 'family' meeting will be less appropriate in an evangelistic setting when we have uninitiated guests present. We need to ask ourselves whether or not worship has a role to play in evangelistic meetings anyway. Do we need to sing for twenty minutes in order to feel the presence of God in a meeting?

The worship leader and team will be more concerned with this aspect. Obviously, ten minutes at the start of a meeting requires far less planning than forty-five minutes.

Another question that we should ask is: why does every meeting have to start with a 'time of worship'? Does everything have to be preceded by singing?

A framework is essential

I have learned that people who are involved in a public event need the security of a framework. They can work better when they know what the expectations are and how they can contribute. Planning our liturgy is not unspiritual. We seek the mind of the Holy Spirit as we do so, using our creative gifts in partnership with Him.

As I have said previously, the Holy Spirit needs to be given the right to change our plans, if He so desires.

Choosing songs

The following list should be a help as you think through the choice of songs for a 'time of worship'.

Use songs that:

1. Complement the theme of the event.
2. Are currently popular with the congregation.
3. Fit in with the direction you want to take the worship.
4. Have a similar emphasis or theme.
5. Fit in with the current emphasis in the church.
6. Flow together, musically or rhythmically.
7. Are new and need to be taught.
8. Have not been used for a while but are relevant again.
9. You enjoy singing.
10. Suit your own voice and style. Maybe they will need to be transposed into a key that suits your voice.

The following guidelines will also be a help to you:

1. **Use variety**. Don't string together a lot of songs that are similar in content and style.
2. **Don't put too many songs into your programme**. I despair whenever I go to a worship event and see a pile of acetates lying by the projector. Something tells me we are going to sing all these songs no matter what happens. We plough through these songs rather than taking time to savour them and meditate on the words. Use fewer songs but get as much out of each as is possible, without 'over-singing' a song.
3. **Lower the keys of some songs**. It is unfortunate that many of the writers of contemporary worship songs are male and write to suit their own vocal range. Most men can sing higher than most women. The women often get frustrated in worship because they struggle to sing these songs. We need to look seriously at lowering the keys of some of our songs.

   Perhaps then we will not only see the women more able to participate but we will see more female worship leaders.
4. **Use a song list**. Have one handy which is divided into three categories: slow, medium and fast. Have the songs listed in alphabetical order and with the keys clearly marked alongside. Keep it handy when you are leading so that it can be referred to as necessary. A thematic index of the same songs is also invaluable.

Creative ideas

The hymn/prayer/hymn/Bible-reading sandwich may be boring. But forty-five minutes of singing can be equally so. Let's employ creative ideas like those listed below. It is not an exhaustive list but I trust it will stimulate your own thoughts.

1. Scripture readings accompanied by music and/or dramatised by actors.
2. Meditative readings used in a similar way.
3. Dramas, dances and mimes, portraying an attribute of God.
4. Poetry.
5. Musicians playing creatively. This ministers to people, provides a background for worship and can release the prophetic gifts (see Chapter 6).
6. Make room for people to sing in the Spirit.
7. Encourage prophecy, spoken and sung.
8. Corporate prayers read out in unison. Praying in small groups for specific needs.
9. An appropriate performance/ministry song.
10. Commence the meeting with teaching/preaching and conclude with worship.

CHAPTER 9

THE WORSHIP LEADER

Over the last decade, there has been a revolution in the way we worship together corporately. The 'new churches' pioneered a new style of worship leading.

Songwriters of contemporary praise and worship songs emerged. These writers were also gifted in leading congregations to express their worship. Major UK events such as Spring Harvest promoted this new model of a 'worship leader and band' leading the congregation in praise.

This style is now being adopted right across the denominational spectrum.

The style may be new, but the concept is not. Every denomination has a way of giving a lead in worship. The Salvation Army have their brass bands, the Anglicans have a choir. When I grew up in the Pentecostal church there would be someone 'leading the choruses'.

The worship leader is an integral part of the local church ministry team. Leadership is needed and recognised at every level of church life, and worship should not be the exception.

The role of the worship leader is to lead the church to worship, when it meets together.

The Old Testament refers to people leading the singing:

1 Chronicles 15:16–27
1 Chronicles 25:1
2 Chronicles 5:12,13
Nehemiah 11:22, 23
Nehemiah 12:8, 42, 46

As in all other areas of church leadership, the role of worship leader can be filled by a woman or a man (Exod. 15:20,21).

It is necessary therefore to look in detail at the hallmarks and the role of a worship leader.

Hallmarks of a worship leader

1. Gifted

Gifting is linked to our call. In the main, God wants us to do what we are good at. A worship leader needs to be gifted in the following ways:

Musically—There must be an appreciation and basic understanding of music.

It is helpful but not essential if the person concerned can play an instrument that gives a rhythmical lead.

Singing—The worship leader needs to be able to sing reasonably in tune.

Leadership—There should be an ability to motivate a congregation to respond in worship. I believe that God equips people specifically to lead worship. It means that something happens when they move in this area of gifting. It is not simply a matter of standing up and introducing songs with a few shouts of 'glory' thrown in. There is a spiritual dynamic in operation when the right person is doing the job.

2. Skilled

a) In music—Being gifted is one thing; developing those gifts is another.

The worship leader should aim to be a master craftsman. In 1 Samuel 16:17 Saul called for a musician, 'someone who plays well'. In 1 Chronicles 15:22, Kenaniah was put in charge of the singing, 'because he was skilful at it'.

Attention should be given to any musical weakness. In areas such as reading music, playing by ear, improvisation and transposition, tuition may be necessary in order to progress.

Better-quality instruments may need to be purchased. Recently, all the singers in the worship team I lead have had voice training. This is enabling them to sing with more control and improved quality.

God is worth the very best when it comes to worship. Let's give Him the highest standard we can. Let's not settle for being second rate, using the phrase 'It's good enough for worship.'

b) In sensitivity—Sensitivity to the Holy Spirit and the congregation is vital. I am filled with despair when I see a worship leader who is oblivious to what God is doing—unaware of the moving of the Holy Spirit in a meeting—or even if aware, still ploughing on with the predetermined course, getting through every song on the programme, especially the current favourite!!

When we lead worship, there should be planning. We cannot come to a meeting unprepared and simply be spontaneous. We could end up with a spontaneous nothing. However, we must be flexible enough to scrap our plans if the Holy Spirit leads us in another direction.

Being skilled in sensitivity is acquired over a period of time: watching others at work and learning from our mistakes; learning to respond to the leading of the Holy Spirit.

Role of a worship leader

1. An example
As someone once said: 'Example is not the best way of teaching somebody, it is the only way.' Leadership demands moral excellence and integrity.

The worship leader and team need to be worshippers, living a lifestyle of worship and leading by the example they set. My own team know that even when they are having a week off and sitting in the congregation, they are to be an example.

People will be watching them to see how they respond when they are not 'out front'. What we are in private determines the effectiveness of our public ministry.

2. A servant

Jesus made it clear that those seeking greatness will be disappointed. Leaders are servants (Mark 10:43). Jesus was an example of this (John 13:5).

Worship leaders serve God and His people. What a privilege this is! It is vital that serving is done without a vested interest. We need to check our motivation. If we only serve in order to gain promotion or recognition, we are heading for disaster. We need to serve with the attitude that says, 'We are happy to do this because God and His people are worth it.'

The leaders of a church need to be confident that a worship leader is not interested solely in fulfilling his/her own agenda, but owning theirs. That way, mutual trust and confidence are built.

3. A pastor

I once heard a story of two friends travelling in the Middle East. They saw a man driving a flock of sheep. One commented that it was strange to see a shepherd driving the flock. 'Surely the shepherd leads the flock,' said one. 'That is not the shepherd,' the other replied. 'He is the butcher!' The role of the worship leader is to be a shepherd to the flock. Sadly, I have seen too many congregations butchered—driven along by a worship leader who criticises their lack of response during worship, insensitive to the reasons for their lack of response. You may have a similar experience.

I seek to draw out the worship that is in people's hearts. I do not want to impose my way of doing things on a congregation. As has been said in an earlier chapter, the Holy Spirit is a gentleman, not a bully. I must endeavour to be the same in the way I exercise my role as worship leader.

4. A prophet
This is the radical side of the worship leader. The pastoral characteristic is held in tension with the prophetic.

Worship leaders should be breaking new ground in worship, both privately and publicly, pioneering so that others may benefit. They should understand what God is currently saying to the church. Their choice of songs should reflect this.

Singing, music and worship unlock the prophetic gifts in a church meeting. The leaders of worship in David's time were prophets and they led God's people in prophetic worship (1 Chron. 25:1–6).

Practical helps

A chapter on the worship leader would be incomplete without some attention given to the practicalities of leading worship.

The following is a helpful guide to the do's and don'ts:

Lead with faith
It is all too easy to rely on a formula for leading worship. For example, two fast songs to get people going, followed by a couple of slow songs which lead into singing in the Spirit. It is far easier to repeat something that has worked well in the past, rather than step into uncharted areas. If we rely on a formula, faith disappears. The Holy Spirit is replaced by professionalism. It is faith that will cause us to please God. Faith is spelt R.I.S.K. A simple question to ask is—when did we last do something for the first time?

Lead with confidence

We need to overcome our fear of making mistakes. Mistakes will be made as we function in the area of our gift. Let us ensure we learn from them. It is essential that our lives and ministries are not ruled by fear—fear of failure, rejection, criticism, etc. Love replaces fear. Let us live in the security of God's love and that of our close friends, believing that God has confidence in us and that others are wanting us to succeed and not fail.

Lead with clarity

People want to be led, so be unafraid to take the initiative. I have never yet encountered a congregation who refuse to stand when I ask them to do so. Do not be hesitant and timid when giving instructions. Neither be like a sergeant-major, bellowing at reluctant conscripts. Strike a balance, leading with courtesy and warmth. An example of this would be: 'Let's all stand and sing together,' as opposed to 'I want you all to stand and sing.'

Use inclusive language. It is all too easy to use words that relate to families to the exclusion of single people.

Lead in a non-religious manner

Do not put on a different voice or manner when leading. Some theological colleges teach trainees how to speak in a religious 'reverent' voice.

Use non-religious vocabulary, speaking in today's language and not that of the eighteenth century.

Dispense with words like 'just', as in 'let's just pray'. It is an unnecessary word. Religiosity is opposed to reality and leads to pretence. Develop a hatred for it.

Lead with your eyes open

Creating a rapport with those whom we are leading requires eye contact. We need to watch how people are responding, otherwise we will end up having our own little meeting. If we are working with a leader/elder who has overall responsibility for the meeting, we need to keep eye contact with that person. If we do not, we will miss out on signals that someone else has a contribution to bring.

Don't worship for too long

I would much rather have five minutes of eternity than fifty minutes that feels like eternity. If the Holy Spirit is moving in a powerful way, time flies by. When nothing like this is happening, let's be flexible enough to end the 'time of worship' early. After about twenty minutes, people start to switch off anyway, unless something unusual is happening. All worship leaders should take the opportunity of occasionally sitting at the back of a meeting and see how people there are responding, especially in prolonged times of worship. Quite often they will be observing what is happening in the front few rows of the congregation.

Don't teach too many new songs

It is good to introduce new songs on a continual basis. One or two during the course of a meeting is the maximum. Be careful where in the programme you do this. I prefer to teach songs at the beginning of a meeting and weave them into the worship later on.

Don't waffle!

The flow of worship is hindered when a worship leader gives a pep talk or mini-preach between the songs. Most worship leaders are not preachers and the anointing is not on them for that. However, the occasional brief (and I mean brief) exhortation is helpful. If doing this, ensure that it is done in a succinct way. Maybe even write down a few headlines before the meeting commences. At all costs avoid falling into sentimentality when speaking between songs.

Watch the volume of the music

People are coming to worship the Lord, not to a rock concert. The music should provide an adequate lead. The congregation should not have to shout to be heard above the band or be deafened by the level of the PA system. Establish who is in charge of the PA and give clear guidelines on required sound-levels.

Make sure people have the lyrics

If using song-sheets, please give out the numbers of the songs. There is nothing more irritating, especially for visitors, than searching vainly through a song-sheet, only finding the song just before it ends. If using an overhead projector, ensure that the lyrics are bold enough to be seen at the rear of the hall, and by everybody. Make sure the operator knows how to use the equipment in an efficient manner. You do not want the congregation gazing at a blank screen.

Use variety

Blend fast and slow songs into the programme—songs that raise the roof and those that are quieter. Make room for silence and meditation. Bringing light and shade into the worship is essential.

Explain what is happening

This is particularly important for those who may be visitors to the church. Do not assume that everyone is initiated into the way things are done. For example, if there is a message in tongues, explain what has happened, in a clear concise way.

When there are unbelievers present, explanation will help them to feel included into the event.

Communicate clearly with musicians

Let them know what songs are likely to be used. Make sure that clear signals are worked out to indicate key changes, changes of tempo and endings of songs. The musicians need to be able to hear the instructions you are giving to the congregation. The worship leader needs clear lines of sight to the music group, particularly those musicians who set the pace, the drummer and leading instruments.

On a final note, there are some excellent seminars

being organised these days. They deal with many of the practical aspects of leading worship and putting teams together. Subscribing to an organisation such as the Christian Music Association (CMA) will enable you to stay informed of such events.

CHAPTER 10

THE WORSHIP TEAM

How to form the team

You may listen to the latest worship album release and feel discouraged. On the recording, there could be a full orchestra and a cast of thousands singing. These songs will not sound anything like the album when you and your small worship team sing them.

You may desire to emulate the quality on these records but with limited skills and resources it will not be possible. Maturity, though, is aiming for the ideal while living with the actual.

You may only have a couple of guitars and a flute player at your disposal. However, it is a good starting point. That is what I started with when I first began to lead in worship. Do the very best you can with the resources you have, while always being on the lookout for new talent.

A big band is not always necessary. I frequently lead at events where there are hundreds of people and all I have is my voice and guitar. What is far more important is that the congregation are being encouraged to come to meetings prepared to give. If the majority of people are 'raring to go' in worship, they will not be bothered by limitations of instruments.

It is true, though, that having a band can make the job a lot easier.

The following guidelines should help as you seek to build a worship team:

1. Establish your musical direction.

What style of music do you want to play?
Once this is decided, begin to look for the
musical resources that will fit into that style.
Do not simply assemble a band from all the
various instruments and musicians available.
Use the right people to obtain the sound you
want to achieve.

2. Develop the resources you already have. Get
   the very best out of them. Arrange singing
   lessons or refresher courses on the instruments.

3. Make your needs for personnel known.
   Advertise in the church news-sheet. You may
   be surprised what hidden talent is waiting to
   be discovered.

4. Build the team gradually with quality people.
   Pray about the sort of people you are looking
   for.

5. As the team grows, give responsibility to key
   people who can be trusted. This ensures you
   won't be getting a nervous breakdown by
   trying to run everything and do every job.

6. Audition those who would like to join the
   team. (This applies more to a larger church.)
   This gives you the chance to assess their level
   of musical competence, character and commitment to the church. Use musicians who are
   already committed to the church. If they are
   only coming to the church because it means
   they can play publicly, you will hit problems
   further on.

7. At the audition spell out what it means to be a
   part of the worship team. Outline your expectations, such as attending rehearsals, reliability,
   being on time, keeping a file of new songs.

Qualities needed in team members

1. A heart for worship

This is the primary requirement of anybody who is involved in a worship team. It does not matter how skilful a musician or singer is. If that person is not a worshipper, they will be a liability. A less able musician who has a heart for worship, is worth ten brilliant musicians who are not worshippers. At my worship team rehearsals, I put a great priority on us worshipping together, often without instruments to hide behind. I impress on my team that we are all worship leaders, musicians and singers alike.

2. Musical skill

I want the music we offer to God to be of the best possible standard. He is worthy of excellence. To be in a worship band is the highest calling for any musician. I do not use the phrase 'it is good enough for worship', to cover sub-standard workmanship by my team. In our teams we may not have musicians and singers who are trained to the highest degree. We may have a few guitarists who know a handful of chords. That is where I started. However, we need to get the very best out of the resources we have. A dedicated average musician is far better than a musical genius who has an attitude of 'anything will do for God'.

3. A desire to serve

Given the opportunity, any musician would love the opportunity of playing before an audience. Does that same musician have a desire to serve in less prestigious roles, for example, putting out the chairs or songbooks? I do not want musicians playing publicly before I am convinced that they are happy to serve. New worship team members in my church spend time operating the overhead projector or helping set up the PA system, before stepping into the limelight. I want them to prove faithful in the small things before trusting them with public profile.

Gift and character

It is so easy to promote someone because they are gifted, especially if they can fulfil a role that is urgently needed.

The problem with gifted people is that unless character has been developed, there will be problems further down the line. I look for both gift and character to be developed in the team I work with.

Someone who has allowed their character to be developed will be teachable and respond well to authority and criticism. They will honour others rather than seek glory for themselves. They will display good attitudes to others. We are not looking for 'doormats' who will do everything we ask without questioning. We are looking for those who will not give us the 'Third World War' every time we make a demand on them.

The PA team

I have noticed how thankless a task it is to be involved in the PA team. The work they do is often not publicly acknowledged. When the sound is good, no one says a word. However, as soon as something goes wrong, they get all the flak. If someone thinks the sound at a meeting is too loud, they lay into the poor sound engineer. I have seen it happen so many times. The way some members of churches treat their sound team is appalling.

I have also observed the conflict that can so easily occur between the sound engineer and the band.

Sometimes they are almost working in competition with each other. There is such a lack of trust and confidence. This is an environment in which nothing good can flourish.

I have responsibility for the PA team in my home church as well as the worship team. These are some of the ideas that have been put into practice in order to promote a better working relationship:

1. A leader is given responsibility for ensuring the sound levels are conducive to worship. This person is present during the sound-check. As a third person, the leader can defuse any tension between the band and the sound engineer.

2. The only person who can make comment to the sound team regarding the 'front of house' sound levels, once the meeting has started, is the leader.

   Any complaints are referred to that person. The sound engineer has strict instructions to point any irate persons towards the leader.

3. When people join the worship team, they spend time working on the PA team. This gives them a greater understanding of the problems that are faced. They also develop a good relationship with the members of the PA team. This helps when they are on the other side of the microphone, at a future date.

4. The worship team and the PA team are one team rather than two separate teams competing against each other.

5. Sound engineers are encouraged to attend rehearsals, so that they can be aware of the musical arrangements to songs. I see a sound engineer as the extra band member. This person may not be on stage, but what he or she does will enhance the quality of the music.

6. Always thank the sound engineer after the event. Even if it has been a bad evening, that person will have given of their best.

Developing the team

It is essential to build the musicians and singers into a good team. A sense of teamwork will enable the job to be done really well.

Why team work?
- It's biblical. Jesus worked within a team. The early church had apostolic teams.
- It's practical. We are more effective together than individually.
- Team is process, not just product—not looking only at the end product but at the process to get us there. Team work enables us to get a job done effectively. However, the process of working together is as important as what we achieve.
- What is seen can only be good if what is unseen is good.

Characteristics of team
- Has a clear purpose. Team leaders need to keep re-affirming/re-defining purpose.
- Has more than one member.
- Needs a structure. Individuals need to know who is leading. They also need to know what their particular role is.
- Needs an environment in which to operate. In this case, the regular church meetings and wherever worship is required.

Characteristics of a good team
- Submissive attitudes to leadership structure.
- Accountability—for example, about delegation.
- Communication—verbal and written.
- Supporting/caring for each other.
- Clear expectations.
- Clear working guidelines.
- Commitment to vision of team.
- Flexibility.
- Unselfishness—individuals willing to lay

down gifting for the good of the team.
- Shared responsibility—we are all in this together.
- Enthusiasm.
- Good relationships, developed through working together and relaxing together.
- Built-in evaluation and feedback/monitoring.
- Individual and corporate development.
- Leadership.
- Good resources and stewardship of resources.

What can a team leader expect of members?
- Input of creative ideas and into the shape of the team.
- Commitment—a willingness to release time, energy and resources to the task and team.
- Sharing of responsibility.
- Co-operation.
- Growth/development in members.
- Serving heart.
- Honesty.
- Supportive environment.
- Conflicts will be faced and worked out.
- Faithfulness—in small things as in large.

What can team members expect of the team leader?
- Encouragement.
- Feedback.
- Education/training.
- Care/support.
- Envisioning/direction.
- Loyalty.
- Clear expectations and being held to them.
- Good communication.
- Honesty.
- Opportunity to be stretched/trained.
- Clear assessment and feedback.
- Respect and approval.
- A listening ear.
- Opportunity to contribute.
- Resources to get the job done.

CHAPTER 11

IMPLEMENTING CHANGE

Having read through this book, you may be asking yourself how you can bring some changes to the public worship in your church.

When things change, we will always find our security threatened. This is why change is always unpopular. I subscribe to a firm belief in 'an experimental approach to church life'. This means that we stick with a way of doing things until it ceases to be effective, or God moves us on. When I first joined Pioneer People (formerly Cobham Christian Fellowship) in 1980, our main church meeting was on a Thursday evening. That left the weekends free for us to spend time with each other as friends, not just relating to each other in meetings. We would close down public meetings in the summer as everyone tended to be on holiday anyway. Eventually we decided that a Sunday evening meeting was the best time to meet, in order to bring a more evangelistic edge.

We used to meet at around 7 p.m. but found that an earlier time was necessary in order to reach families. We constantly review everything we are doing in the light of our goals as a church. We implement change where necessary. We believe constant change is here to stay. We want to move when God moves and stop when He stops. In 1992 we realised our name needed to change as we no longer held our main church meeting in Cobham. Indeed, we have a vision to evangelise the area beyond Cobham. The name Pioneer People (a church in the community), seemed appropriate in the light of what we are—pioneers, not settlers, and because we care about people.

Most churches do not operate on this basis. They do the same thing, week in, week out. The name above the door indicates where the vision ceased.

My colleague Gerald Coates talked to a minister at a recent large Christian event. The minister was so stirred up by what he had seen God doing that he stated he was going back to his church to 'drag them into the twentieth century'. Gerald replied that he had better hurry up as there were only seven years of the twentieth century left!

I am often asked to give seminars on worship leading. Whenever I give an opportunity for questions, I always get these two:

1. 'Can you give me some advice as to how I can bring changes to the way we worship in my home church? How can new songs be introduced, and greater room be given for the Holy Spirit to move?'
2. 'We as a worship group want to move the church on in worship, but people are reluctant to change. Some have threatened to leave the church if we introduce livelier songs and a variety of instruments. What can we do?'

I answer the first in this way:

a) It is vital to give clear communication of why change is needed. Without it there is always room for misunderstanding and a risk of losing people.

    It will be necessary to give some teaching on praise and worship to the whole church. Maybe some creative worship workshops will need to be organised so that people can learn in a practical way. There may be a fear of the supernatural working of the Holy Spirit which will need handling in a sensitive manner.

b) It can take a couple of years to implement major change in a church. There are practical implications that will need to be addressed. We cannot change the way a congregation worships overnight. The order of service may not have changed in fifty years. So we need patience while we move gradually from the old to the new. Maturity is aiming for the ideal while being content with the actual.

c) Wherever possible we must maintain unity and deal lovingly with each other. Bear in mind that change is often implemented by a small group before it breaks out into the main congregation.

d) Effective change is facilitated when enough people feel dissatisfied with the way things are.

I answer the second in this way:

a) The reluctance to change in worship is symptomatic of a more serious problem. Worship is the tip of the iceberg. The real problem is that the church does not want to change anything.

Those who are resistant to change in worship will probably be reluctant to evangelise their area and have no vision for anything other than maintaining the status quo.

b) Leaders must lead. The tail does not wag the head. If the leadership of a church wants to move the church forward, they should be able to do so without the 'Third World War' taking place. Leaders need to communicate their vision in such a way that as many people as possible eagerly buy into it. Those who do not can always find another church to meet their needs. Should someone threaten to leave a church if the worship changes, let them leave. We should not pander to 'blackmail' and threats.

c) If you are in a church that is not open to God

changing things, find one that is. We have only got one life. Why waste it propping up a church that has no vision to get God's will done?

In our worship, there will be a blend of old and new. We need to be radical conservatives—moving forward radically in our worship, while conserving the best of what has been in the past.

The worship life of a church will reflect its vision or lack of it. Worship is either prophetic or nostalgic!

BETTER THAN OR EQUAL TO?

A Look at Singleness

Linda Harding

This three-part study in the Pioneer *Perspectives* series is a look at the significance of single people, both individually and as groups. Singleness as a topic leads to many interesting and varied questions and author Linda Harding addresses the role of the church as the pacesetter, responding to changing demographics and increasing numbers of single adults.

To be single in the 1990s requires faith and an understanding of God's calling and courage to walk in it. This is the decade when the church has an opportunity to be God's provision of prophetic community, with a radical challenging message.

The reader is helped to understand the biblical perspective on singleness. The book stimulates and raises the level of awareness of attitudes and issues relating to singleness and of the needs and potential of single people. It can be used as an aid to envision and equip the church, to help it respond creatively, positively and practically to this significant group of people.

Catalogue Number YB 9729   £3.99

PROPHECY IN THE CHURCH

Martin Scott

At key times prophecy can shape your life. It is a gift which can radically change the course of a person's life or even that of a nation. Helping, inspiring and blessing, the individual is touched by words from the very Father heart of God, spoken to you as an individual or to the church as the body of Christ.

This book in the Pioneer *Perspectives* series is primarily concerned with the gift of prophecy and also the role and ministry of the prophet, leading one to ask:

Does this affect me?

Can the Holy Spirit really dwell within me?

Should I be expectant and desire change and challenge?

Martin Scott clearly states the Holy Spirit does reside in the Christian and He can manifest Himself through you at the right time in a variety of situations. Prophecy happens because God is a person who speaks. It is simply one of the things that the Holy Spirit does when He is free to do as He wishes.

This book is a sound study aid as we learn to be aware of and expectant for the Holy Spirit. Prophecy is a gift which we should expect to be poured out liberally during the age of the Holy Spirit. So much so, that Paul expected us to 'eagerly desire spiritual gifts, especially the gift of prophecy' *(1 Cor. 14:1)*.

Catalogue Number YB 9726   £3.99

RADICAL EVANGELISM

A New Look at an Old Commission

Pete Gilbert

This Pioneer *Perspective* gives the biblical basis for the theology of evangelism, resting on the contention that God wants to communicate to His people of all time, all of the time.

Pete Gilbert reiterates the words of Paul to Colosse and clearly explains the role of the 20th-century church and its people to 'proclaim the mystery of Christ' with clarity, wisdom and grace.

Therefore the role of the evangelist, as pointed out by this *Perspective* and Paul's words, is to pass on the good news and to equip and train others to do likewise.

The author writes that in the sphere of radical evangelism, plans need to be created and implemented. Pete Gilbert suggests a 5-point strategy that includes commitment, development, research, action and persistence, which are all fully explained in turn, and a handy help to any church wanting to grow in this decade of evangelism.

Catalogue Number YB 9728   £3.99

RELATIONSHIPS— JESUS STYLE

Stuart Lindsell

For many of us, it is in the area of relationships that we feel the most insecure. Relating to God is not too bad, but relationships with people can be fraught with difficulties and misunderstanding.

This Pioneer *Perspective* is therefore focused on a word of instruction that Jesus spoke to His disciples about their relationships together. Jesus, by His words, His lifestyle of love, acceptance and forgiveness, His faith in his church and purity in His relationships, is our great example. Jesus also recognised His own need of others despite His unique relationship with the Father.

This useful book gives guidance to all of us in creating and maintaining relationships within the church. The biblical teaching is logical and here we have a powerful aid to uniting the church by building strong relationships based on love, acceptance, trust and respect.

Catalogue Number YB 9727   £3.99

THE ROLE AND MINISTRY OF WOMEN

Martin Scott

This two-part study in the Pioneer *Perspectives* series is the result of faithful research into an emotive subject: the role of women in the church – specifically in relation to their ministry as leaders. In a topic of heated debate the author has related the role women should play in the light of the revelation of God found within His Word.

The author points out that the Gospel comes to liberate regardless of differing perspectives; it makes us into the men and women God wants us to be. In Christ there is full and equal redemption for all people regardless of race, gender or social background *(Gal. 3:28)*.

So, how can women best be freed to serve effectively as God wants? If there are questions which remain, let us deal with each other graciously, knowing that God is always willing to shed more light where we are seeking answers, which will help us continue to walk in integrity before Him.

Catalogue Number YB 9725 £3.99